ALEXANDER
THE GREAT

Copyright © 2005 Marshall Editions

Conceived, edited and designed by Marshall Editions
The Old Brewery, 6 Blundell Street, London N7 9BH
www.quarto.com

First published in the UK in 2005 by
QED Publishing
A division of Quarto Publishing plc
226 City Road
London EC1V 2TT

A Catalogue record for this book is available from the British Library.

ISBN 1 84538 203 X

Originated in Hong Kong by Modern Age
Printed and bound in China by Midas Printing Limited

For Marshall Editions:
Publisher: Richard Green
Commissioning editor: Claudia Martin
Art direction: Ivo Marloh
Editor: Sharon Hynes
Picture manager: Veneta Bullen
Production: Anna Pauletti

Design: Tall Tree
Cover: QED Publishing
Series editor: Miranda Smith
Project editor: Paula Borton
Picture research: Caroline Wood

Consultant: Paul Cartledge is Professor of Greek History at the University of Cambridge, England.

Previous page: Alexander the Great depicted as Helios Kosmokrator, the sun god.
Opposite: Alexander fights the Persians, as shown on a contemporary sarcophagus.

ALEXANDER
THE GREAT

THE BOY SOLDIER WHO CONQUERED THE WORLD

SIMON ADAMS

QED

CONTENTS

THE BOY FROM MACEDON

Birth of a Prince   8
Macedon   10
The Royal Parents   12
Bucephalas   14
Two Tests of Manhood   16

THE YOUNG KING

Alexander the Man   20
Aristotle the Teacher   22
Becoming King   24
Wives and Friends   26
The Lord of Asia   28

CONQUERING
THE WORLD

Into Asia and Africa   32
Alexander's Campaigns   36
Becoming a God   38
Into Persia   40
Into India   44

3

THE END OF
HIS WORLD

Return from India   50
Death of a Conqueror   54
Where Is Alexander Buried?   56
The Legacy of Alexander   58

Glossary   60
Bibliography and Index   62

4

THE BOY FROM
MACEDON

Birth of a Prince

In 356 B.C., a baby boy was born in Pella, the capital of Macedon, which was a kingdom of ancient Greece. His mother was Olympias, a queen of Macedon. The boy's father, King Philip II, had already been married three times and was later to marry three more times. He had other children, but this son, Alexander, was special for he was to become one of the few people in history to be called 'the Great'.

When Alexander was born, his father was on a military campaign in the south of his country and had just captured an important town. The Greek historian Plutarch records that three messages reached King Philip at the same time. The first told him that one of his generals, Parmenion, had just won a great victory over Macedon's historic enemies, the Illyrians. The second said that one of his racehorses had won at the Olympic Games. The third said that a son had been born to him.

Previous page: Like this young Greek boy, Alexander was vigorous and healthy.

Left: The mythical Heracles – better known to us by his Roman name, Hercules – was the son of the god Zeus. Brave and strong, he carried out 12 famous labours. Alexander's father claimed to be descended from Heracles.

Due to the problem of precisely dating some events in Alexander's life, some of the dates given are approximate. 'c.' is an abbreviation of 'circa', meaning 'about'.

382 B.C.
Philip, son of King Amyntas III of Macedon, is born.

Most of what we know about Alexander's early life comes from the biography written by Plutarch some 400 years after his birth. Alexander was born at a time of great military success for his father and his country, and at a time of great sporting success against other Greek states. The name Philip and Olympias chose for him, Alexander, was common in the Macedonian royal house. It was also the other name that the legendary Trojan hero Paris was called by in stories about the Trojan Wars, written down by the Greek poet Homer in the *Iliad*.

Both of Alexander's parents claimed that they were descended from mythical great heroes of ancient Greece – Philip from Heracles, son of the god Zeus, and Olympias from Achilles, one of the heroes of the Trojan Wars. The ancient Greeks saw Alexander's birth as no normal event. He was a boy born to the descendants of gods and heroes, and destined for greatness.

The first Olympics

The first Olympic Games are believed to have been held around 776 B.C. at Olympia in southern Greece. By the fifth century B.C., the games took place over five days every four years. They included running, wrestling, horse riding and chariot racing. On the last day, the winners were awarded wreaths of olive leaves.

Right: Achilles was one of the Greek heroes of the Trojan Wars. Alexander's mother, Olympias, claimed she was descended from him.

359 B.C.
Philip seizes the throne from his nephew and rules Macedon as Philip II.

357 B.C.
Philip marries Olympias of Molossia, who becomes his fourth wife.

Macedon

The kingdom that Alexander inherited, Macedon, was to the north of the main Greek city-states such as Athens and Sparta. The country was once divided between the mountainous Upper Macedon in the west and the more fertile Lower Macedon in the east. The two halves were united by Alexander's father, Philip. Although the Macedonians spoke Greek, their dialect contained so many foreign words that many Greeks did not consider Macedonians to be Greek at all. As a result, many Greeks disliked Alexander. They saw him as a foreigner.

Right: When Alexander's father, Philip, took the throne of Macedon in 359 B.C. it was a powerful but divided city-state. He set about unifiying it before beginning his conquest of the other city-states of ancient Greece, which lay to the south.

PHILIP'S MACEDON

ILLYRIA
Philippopolis • THRACE
Byzantium
Stageira
MACEDON • Pella
Mieza • Olynthus
Aegae
HELLESPONT
Mt. Olympus
CHALCIDICE • Troy
EPIRUS
THESSALY
Aegean Sea
MOLOSSIA
IONIA
Thebes • Ephesus
Delphi •
Chaeronea • Athens
Olympia • Corinth
Argos • Miletus
Halicarnassus
Sparta
RHODES
N
W ··· E
CRETE
S

Main picture: The west of Macedon was covered with rugged mountains and lush valleys, warm in summer but bitterly cold in winter. The east of Macedon was flatter, with large fertile plains and gently rolling hills.

UNIQUE ARMY

Alexander was not the first in his family to be a great military commander. He inherited the superb army that his father had created. As was usual, it was made up of cavalry (on horses) and infantry (on foot). But the way Philip organized his soldiers made his army unique. The Companion Cavalry was made up of the nobility and wealthy landowners. By their side fought the Macedonian Foot Companions, full-time soldiers who were heavily armed. These fighters were trained to react quickly.

Right: Macedonian infantry used a *sarissa*, **or long pike, to attack the enemy before they got within stabbing range.**

Above: Alexander and Philip were born in the palace of the capital of Macedon, Pella. Today the palace is in ruins, but once it had splendid mosaic floors and columned rooms.

The Royal Parents

Alexander's parents were both strong and forceful characters. Not surprisingly, their marriage was stormy. Alexander often found himself caught up in the crossfire between the two.

Philip was not meant to become king of Macedon, because he was not his father's oldest son. But when his older brother Perdiccas III died in 359 B.C., Philip was made regent for his nephew – Perdiccas' underage son and successor, Amyntas. Philip was not content to rule only until the boy reached adulthood. He seized the throne himself and then began a series of wars, conquering his neighbours and greatly increasing his territory.

Greece was not then the united nation it is today. It was a collection of independent states that often fought against each other. The most powerful of these states had been Athens, Sparta and Thebes. Under Philip, Macedon fought its way to the top and became the most powerful state in all Greece.

Above: Alexander's father, Philip II of Macedon, was buried in a splendid tomb in Vergina, once known as Aegae, the original capital of Macedon. This ivory statue was found when the tomb was excavated during the 1970s.

c. 20 July 356 B.C.
Alexander is born in Pella, capital of Macedon. He is the son of Philip and Olympias.

356 B.C.
The Third Sacred War breaks out in Greece over the control of the sacred shrine of Delphi.

In order to increase his power, Philip also used marriage as an effective weapon. He married foreign princesses in order to lessen his enemies' resistance to Macedonian rule or to keep them quiet after their defeat. One such marriage was to Olympias, a Greek princess from Molossia in Epirus, southwest of Macedon. The marriage was also at first a love match, but Philip soon fell out of love with her.

Olympias was a strong woman. Quarrelsome and fiery, she demanded respect. In later life, when Alexander was king, he complained about her attempts to organize his life. When Philip put Olympias aside and married again, she made sure that Alexander remained at

Above: Discovered in Philip's tomb, this breastplate is made of iron with gold decoration. It was possibly worn by Philip in battle.

her side, even though this distanced him from his strict father. Philip had an older son by a previous wife, but Alexander was determined to become king when his father died.

Left: Alexander's mother was a glamorous queen, but had a cruel streak to her character. This portrait comes from a gold medallion unearthed in Egypt.

352 B.C.
Philip seizes control of Thessaly, to the south of Macedon.

348 B.C.
Philip destroys Olynthus, capital of Chalcidice, giving him access to the gold and silver mines of the region.

Bucephalas

In 344 B.C., when he was 12 years old, Alexander met one of his best and most loyal friends. This friend was to be with him for almost 20 years, through battles and sports. His friend had an unusual name – Bucephalas, meaning 'ox-head' – for Bucephalas was not a man but a horse.

The grassy plains of Thessaly, south of Macedon, are famous for wild horses. Bucephalas was especially magnificent, a black stallion with a white blaze on his forehead in the shape of an ox's head. He was, however, highly strung. And no one had 'broken him', which meant that he would not allow anyone to ride him. A horse dealer offered Bucephalas to Philip for the great sum of 13 silver talents. In Alexander's day, a skilled workman only made about two to three drachmas a day, and there were 6,000 drachmas to each talent. That worker would have had to slave away for up to 100 years before he could afford this horse.

Right: Alexander tames Bucephalas, whose name means 'ox-head'. This description may have come from the white mark on the horse's black forehead. Or it may possibly have come from the mark branded onto all horses of his breed.

c. 348 B.C.
Leonidas, a relative of Alexander's mother, takes charge of his education.

346 B.C.
The Peace of Philocrates brings the Third Sacred War to an end with victory for Macedon.

> '*My son, ask for yourself another kingdom,*
> *for that which I leave is too small for you.*'
> **Philip to his son Alexander on his taming of Bucephalas**

Philip refused to buy the horse, but the 12-year-old Alexander intervened. He had noticed that the horse was scared by the sight of its own shadow. He seized the reins and turned the horse's head away from its shadow. He stood next to the horse, stroking him gently and gradually calming him down. After a while, he jumped on the horse's back and rode off across the plain. From then on only Alexander could ride him.

Bucephalas stayed by Alexander's side for 18 years, serving his master both as warhorse and hunter. But in 326 B.C., during the battle of the River Hydaspes in the Punjab in modern Pakistan, Bucephalas was injured and died shortly afterwards. Alexander personally led his horse's funeral procession and buried the animal with great honours. At or near the spot where Bucephalas died, Alexander built a city named Bucephala after his companion. Unfortunately, no trace of this city has ever been found.

Famous horses

The Roman emperor Caligula wanted to make his horse a consul. The English king Richard III offered to give up his kingdom for a horse so that he could escape certain death on the battlefield. But in all history, only Alexander named a city after his horse.

346 B.C.
The Greek writer Isocrates writes *Philippus*, calling on Philip of Macedon to lead a Greek crusade against Persia.

c. 345 B.C.
Alexander is educated by Lysimachus and other teachers.

Two Tests of Manhood

As Alexander grew up, he had to prove himself a worthy successor to his father as king. He did this by taking the two tests every prince of Macedon had to pass before he could be considered grown up.

The two tests were challenging. First, he had to kill a wild boar, and second, kill a man in combat. Once he had achieved these tasks, Alexander would be recognized as a man and could wear a special belt to show this. He would also be able to lie back rather than sit upright at the symposia – the all-male parties that were common at the Macedonian court.

Below: Wild boars were common in the Macedonian mountains. When Alexander, seen here, killed one, he had completed one of the two traditional tests of manhood.

344 B.C.
Alexander tames Bucephalas, a wild Thessalian stallion.

343 B.C.
Philip appoints Aristotle as Alexander's tutor.

Left: Alexander's second test was to kill a man in battle. He is seen here demonstrating his skill in combat.

Alexander killed a wild boar with ease, and from then on became a keen hunter, fighting lions, bears and other wild animals. It was probably not until he was at least 14 years old that he had the chance to kill a man in battle. His victim was to be the first of many.

From Plutarch, we learn other things about the young Alexander. He enjoyed drama and poetry; he learned to play two musical instruments, the lyre and the aulos; he was fond of stick fighting; and he was a fast runner. Plutarch also tells us that Alexander's early education was placed in the hands of Leonidas, a relative of his mother. Leonidas was strict and, in many ways, acted like a foster-father to Alexander, whose real father, Philip, was often away. But Alexander was fonder of another teacher, Lysimachus, even though he was not, according to Plutarch, a 'cultivated' or 'educated' man.

A men's evening

A typical symposium took place after the evening meal had ended. Up to 30 men attended – no women were allowed – each wearing a garland and lying on a couch on his left elbow. Discussion ranged from politics to love, and wine was served. Prayers brought events to a close. The men then paraded drunkenly through the streets before going to bed.

342 B.C. Philip conquers a city in neighbouring Thrace and renames it Philippopolis.	**c. 342–340** B.C. Alexander passes the two Macedonian tests of manhood.

THE YOUNG
KING

2

Alexander the Man

Even though he was still only in his mid-teens, once Alexander had passed his tests of manhood, he was considered to be a man. He had worked hard to acquire the skills he would need both as a man and as the king he hoped to become. But what sort of young man was Alexander?

Previous page: Despite its broken nose, this marble bust shows just how handsome Alexander was.

Sculptures of Alexander show that he was a very handsome young man who was strong and fit, if not very tall. His bravery grew day by day, and he had become a fine hunter and horseman.

Below: Like most powerful people in Greece at the time, Alexander visited Delphi to consult the priestess of the oracle. People believed that she could predict the future, and Alexander was eager to know what it had in store for him. Her shrine was near this temple, which today is in ruins.

341 B.C.
Athenian politician Demosthenes calls for all Greeks to unite against the growing power of Macedon.

340 B.C.
Alexander is made regent while Philip is away at the siege of Byzantium.

Kings-only race

Alexander was such a fast runner that it was suggested he compete in the Olympic Games. He agreed, provided that he only raced against other kings, as only they would be worthy of competing against him.

He had also learned the military skills of using a sword, javelin and bow.

Alexander was extremely intelligent and inquisitive about the world around him. When he was about seven, in his father's absence he had met a group of envoys from Persia, the long-time enemy of the Greek states. He had questioned them closely about their homeland: how far was it to the Persian capital, were the roads good, how big was the army? These were not the questions of an innocent boy marvelling at the strange wonders and mysteries of the east. They were the questions of a clever young man finding out things that he could use later on in his campaigns.

Alexander had gained a lifelong interest in religion, mysticism and superstition from his mother. Olympias was a priestess of the god Dionysus, whose sacred rites were mysterious and wild. She was able to go into a trance and even handled dangerous snakes, which she kept as pets. From her, Alexander inherited his passion and strong will. From his father, Philip, he inherited a hard-headed, realistic approach to life, great personal courage and the ability to make the right decision quickly. It was this mix of skills that was to make Alexander such an extraordinary man.

'Young man, you are invincible!'

Words of the Pythia, the priestess of the oracle at Delphi, to Alexander

340 B.C.
Alexander defeats the Thracian Maedi on Macedon's eastern border.

339 B.C.
Philip gains control of the whole of neighbouring Thrace.

Aristotle the Teacher

In 343 B.C., when Alexander was
13, his father, Philip, appointed
a new tutor to educate his son.
He chose Aristotle, one of the
foremost Greek philosophers of
his day. Aristotle was born in
Stageira in Thrace, east of
Macedon, in 384 B.C. He
spent most of his adult
life in Athens before
being summoned to
educate Alexander at
Mieza. Aristotle was most
interested in science,
particularly botany and
zoology, and passed
on his enthusiasm to the
young man. In later life,
Alexander became
fascinated by the exotic
plants and animals that
he saw in Asia. He sent
specimens to Aristotle, who
by that time was teaching
in Athens. Aristotle also
instructed Alexander in
politics and ethics (morals),
both of which would be useful
when he became king.

**Right: Aristotle (384–
322 B.C.) was a thinker
who inspired people with
his intellect and common
sense. This marble statue
shows him in a typically thoughtful mood.**

TROJAN WARS

Aristotle gave Alexander his own text of a famous poem called the *Iliad*, written on a papyrus scroll. The *Iliad* was written by the Greek poet Homer and told the story of the Trojan Wars between Greece and the city of Troy. The wars were begun by the abduction of the Greek queen Helen by Paris, son of King Priam of Troy. Alexander was fascinated and kept the scroll all his life.

Above: Alexander tried to model himself on some of the Greek heroes that he read about, including Achilles. During the Trojan Wars, according to Homer in the *Iliad*, the Greek hero Achilles came out to fight when his best friend Patroclus was killed. On the vase above, Patroclus is shown lying dead on the ground.

IN HONOUR

It is possible that Alexander was so grateful to Aristotle that he ordered a statue, or bust, of him to be erected in Athens. Although the bust no longer exists, it may once have rested on this later stone pillar. It reads: 'Alexander set up this portrait of the divine Aristotle, the son of Nikomachos, fountain of all wisdom.'

Becoming King

In 340 B.C., Alexander became regent while his father was away. He was only 16 years old, but he more than proved himself as both an able ruler and a daring military commander. Four years later, in suspicious circumstances, Alexander himself became king. His adventure was well under way.

In 340 B.C., Philip led a military campaign against two eastern Greek cities, Byzantium and Perinthus. In his absence, Alexander was made regent. He could have simply ruled Macedon efficiently from the royal palace at Pella. Instead, eager to see some action, he organized his own army to attack and defeat the Thracian Maedi on Macedon's eastern border. In 339 B.C. war broke out between Macedon and the powerful Greek city-state of Athens. Finally, a year later, Philip defeated Greek forces led by Athens and Thebes at the Battle of Chaeronea. Alexander helped by commanding the Macedonian Cavalry.

Left: Philip's decisive victory over the Greeks at Chaeronea in 338 B.C. is marked today by a large statue of a lion, erected on the spot where 300 Theban fighters died in battle.

339 B.C.
The Fourth Sacred War starts between the city-state of Athens and Macedon.

338 B.C.
Philip defeats Greek forces led by Athens and Thebes at Chaeronea. He controls the whole of Greece.

'*What are possessions to me if I achieve nothing?*'
Alexander in 336 B.C., shortly before his father's death

He proved his bravery by leading a decisive charge. Afterwards, Alexander led the guard of honour that returned the ashes of the dead enemy soldiers to their home city of Athens. This was of huge significance. What Philip was really saying to the Greeks about Alexander was: 'Here is your future ruler.'

After his massive victory, Philip was the political and military master of all Greece. He set up the League of Corinth to unite the many Greek states under his leadership. He also began to plan a major expedition against the Persian Empire as revenge for its invasion of Greece in 480–79 B.C. He wanted to free those Greeks still under Persian control in Asia Minor (in modern-day Turkey). But, at only 46 years of age, Philip was assassinated.

At the wedding of his daughter, Cleopatra (Alexander's only full sister), one of Philip's bodyguards, Pausanias, killed him. But did Pausanias act on his own? Many people thought that Olympias was responsible. Some even thought Alexander was to blame, for, since Philip had now chosen him as his successor, he was the one who benefited the most. Whatever happened, the result was clear. At age 20, Alexander became King Alexander of Macedon and ruler of all Greece.

A personal city
After Alexander defeated the Maedi, he created a new Greek-style city on the site of their former capital, naming it Alexandroupolis, the first of many such cities he named after himself.

338 B.C.
Philip establishes the League of Corinth and is chosen to lead the Panhellenic expedition against the Persian Empire.

336 B.C.
Philip is assassinated at his daughter's wedding in Aegae. Alexander becomes king as Alexander III.

Wives and Friends

As soon as he became king, Alexander took steps to secure his position.
He killed all his political opponents and possible rivals to the throne.
But he spared the life of his half-brother, Philip Arrhidaeus, who was
mentally ill. He also got the support of the army and went south to
confirm his leadership of the League of Corinth as his father's successor.
The next step was for him to marry to gain land and make allies.

Alexander was only to marry three times during his life, far fewer than his
father. Alexander's first wife, Roxane, was the beautiful daughter of the

chieftain Oxyartes, whose
lands, in Sogdiana, lay in
Alexander's path as he
travelled eastwards out of
Persia into India. The couple
married in 327 B.C., when
Alexander was 29. Roxane
bore him a son, who would
later become Alexander IV.

Left: Alexander's lifelong friend
Hephaestion is shown here on
the left making an offering at a
shrine. A priestess receives him.
The inscription to this sculpture
reads, 'To Hephaestion, a hero.'

336 B.C.
Darius III becomes King of Persia.

336 B.C.
A combined Macedonian and Greek
army under Parmenion establishes
a foothold in Asia Minor.

Voting for a king

Alexander did not officially become king until the Macedonian army elected him to the job, just as they had elected his father before him.

The marriage to Roxane was at least partly a diplomatic arrangement, like Philip's marriages. So, too, were the two marriages that Alexander contracted in Susa, Persia, in 324 B.C. One of these was to Stateira, one of the daughters of the defeated and assassinated Darius III of Persia. The other marriage was to Parysatis, a daughter of Artaxerxes III, one of Darius' predecessors.

For Alexander, male friends were far more important than wives. His closest and most trusted friend was Hephaestion, whom he met as a boy while studying with Aristotle. Hephaestion stayed at Alexander's side as his bodyguard, principal adviser and, later, Grand Vizier of his empire. Hephaestion died in Ecbatana (in modern-day Iran) in 324 B.C., and Alexander buried him with great ceremony.

His other close friend was a young Persian boy, Bagoas, whom Alexander met in 330 B.C., and who remained close to him throughout his life. These two friendships meant much to him, but Alexander was really a loner who searched for adventure and conquest, not love.

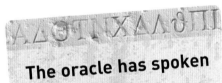

The oracle has spoken

When Hephaestion died, Alexander asked the priest of the oracle of Amun in Egypt how his friend should be remembered. The oracle instructed that Hephaestion should be worshipped as a hero rather than as a god.

---

336 B.C.
Alexander is officially recognized as king by the Macedonian army.

Late summer 336 B.C.
Alexander is recognized as head of the League of Corinth and leader of the expedition against Persia.

The Lord of Asia

As head of the League of Corinth, Alexander had inherited his father's role as leader of the Greek expedition against Asia's mighty Persian Empire. But according to legend, Alexander would have to untie a 'magic' knot, known as the Gordian knot, before he could become master of Asia. First, however, he had business to attend to closer to home.

After Philip's death, some of the territories bordering Macedon rebelled. Alexander acted with speed, striking east against the rebellious Triballi of Thrace, and then north across the River Danube against the Paeonians. This extended Macedonian borders far beyond the area Philip had controlled. Alexander then turned west to defeat the hostile Illyrians.

Macedon itself was now secure, but the Greek partners in the League of Corinth were not so reliable. Acting on the false rumour that Alexander had been killed while on campaign, a number of Greek states, led by Thebes, rose in revolt. Within two weeks, Alexander was at the gates of Thebes, having covered 300 miles in just 12 days. Thebes soon fell to the Macedonian army, and Alexander decided to teach the Thebans – and other potential rebels – a cruel lesson. He killed 6,000 Thebans and sold 30,000 more into slavery. Greece was firmly under Alexander's control.

A terrible tyrant?

Alexander was often merciless to his enemies, and even to his friends. Many historians think he was cruel and unstable. Others think his actions were not shocking by the standards of his time.

Spring 335 B.C.	Summer 335 B.C.
Alexander extends Macedonian power north to the River Danube.	Alexander's army defeats the Illyrians to the west.

> 'What difference does it make how I loose it?'
> **Alexander in Gordium before slashing open the 'magical' knot**

Alexander was now ready to embark on the greatest adventure of his life. In spring 334 B.C., he set sail across the narrow Hellespont waterway that separated Greece from Persian-controlled Asia. As he approached land, he threw his spear into the ground and leapt ashore in full armour. Alexander did not know it yet but a year later, in the city of Gordium to the east, he was to undo the Gordian knot. This knot bound the yoke of a ceremonial wagon to a tall pole. The ends of the knot were tucked away so that it was impossible to untie. It was believed that whoever managed to untie the knot would become the master of Asia. Alexander simply drew his sword and slashed the knot open with a single stroke. The conqueror of Asia had arrived.

Right: Alexander cuts through the Gordian knot with a single stroke.

October 335 B.C.
Alexander captures and destroys the city of Thebes.

Spring 334 B.C.
Alexander sets sail across the Hellespont to reach Asia.

CONQUERING
THE WORLD

Into Asia and Africa

When Alexander landed in Asia in 334 B.C., he was still only 21, and had been King of Macedon for less than two years. Ahead of him lay the conquest of the Persian Empire that he desired, with many battles and famous victories. But his landing in Asia also marked another turning-point in his life – he was never again to see his native land.

Above: Alexander bears down on King Darius at the Battle of Issus. This Roman mosaic from Pompeii, Italy, was made during the 1st century B.C. and is a copy of a painting done a generation after Alexander's death.

Previous page: Alexander rides Bucephalas into combat against the Persians.

Persia's king, Darius III, had, like Alexander, only been king for two years. His empire ran from the Mediterranean Sea east to modern-day Pakistan, and from the Aral Sea in the north to Egypt in the south. Alexander wanted to conquer all of it. The first main battle between the Macedonians and Persians took place at the River Granicus, just east of Troy. Alexander's army of 43,000 infantry and 6,100 cavalry outnumbered the Persian army of 16,000 infantry and 15,000 cavalry. Alexander crossed the river far from the main Persian force, making their commander, Arsites, move his cavalry away from the centre to defend his left wing.

May 334 B.C.
Alexander wins the Battle of the River Granicus.

Summer 334 B.C.
Alexander besieges and captures Miletus and Halicarnassus, two Greek cities on the coast of Asia Minor.

A little bird told him

Alexander was superstitious. At the siege of Halicarnassus, a sparrow perched on his head and refused to move. His personal seer said that this meant a friend was about to betray him, so Alexander had that friend killed.

This left the Persian army overstretched and vulnerable to Alexander's attack.

Although victory eventually went to Alexander, he was nearly killed by Spithridates, satrap of Ionia, who stunned him with an axe. Spithridates was about to deliver the final blow when Cleitus, brother of Alexander's childhood nurse, saved the king by slicing off the Persian's arm.

After the battle, Alexander moved down the Aegean coast of Asia Minor. Most Greek cities welcomed him, glad to be liberated from Persian rule. However, two cities, Miletus and Halicarnassus, refused to surrender and were besieged and captured. Alexander's second big battle was against the Persians at Issus, just where the Mediterranean coastline turns sharply south toward Phoenicia (modern-day Lebanon and coastal Israel).

This time the Persian force was commanded by King Darius himself, and was far larger than Alexander's army. As before, Alexander's well-trained army was superior, and once again the Persians were defeated. Darius fled, leaving behind his mother, wife and two daughters, as well as vast amounts of treasure.

Above: Darius in his chariot turns in fear as Alexander hurtles toward him. Soon after this crushing event, Darius fled from the battlefield.

Spring 333 B.C.
Alexander slashes open the Gordian knot. Legend held that now he would go on to conquer all of Asia.

November 333 B.C.
Alexander wins the decisive Battle of Issus against the Persians.

After Issus, Alexander moved south again, capturing more coastal cities. His plan was to defeat the vast Persian fleet by capturing its bases on land, thus denying it the chance to attack his forces in the rear, perhaps by invading Macedon itself. This plan nearly unravelled at Tyre, a city built on an island near the coast. When Tyre refused to surrender, Alexander built a causeway to the island to attack it. When this was destroyed, he built another. Eventually he managed to attack the island from the seaward side with the help of some rebel Phoenician warships. Alexander chose not to use the Greek fleet to assault Tyre or to attack the Persian navy. This was because the main part of the Greek fleet was Athenian, and Alexander believed that Athenians could not be trusted to remain loyal. He finally captured Tyre after a seven-month siege.

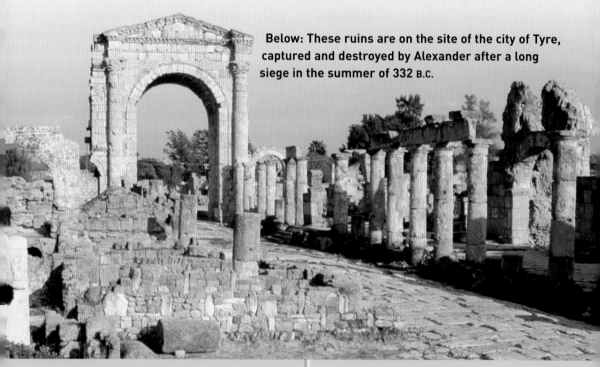

Below: These ruins are on the site of the city of Tyre, captured and destroyed by Alexander after a long siege in the summer of 332 B.C.

January–July 332 B.C.
Alexander besieges and captures Tyre.

September 332 B.C.
Alexander besieges Gaza and later kills its Arab governor.

> *For Alexander, 'the sheer pleasure of battles, as other pleasures are to other men, was irresistible.'*
>
> The 2nd-century A.D. Roman historian Arrian, Alexander's biographer

Alexander then crucified a large number of the people of Tyre on the shoreline to warn others who refused to surrender.

With Tyre safely in his hands, Alexander continued to move south, capturing Gaza after a long siege. As a lesson to others, he ordered its captured Arab governor to be tied to a chariot and dragged around the city walls until he died. Alexander then turned west into Egypt, prized both for its important location and for its vast wealth of gold, grain and other goods. The Egyptians welcomed him as their liberator from Persian rule.

Alexander showed respect for Egyptian traditions and made himself popular by making sacrifices to the sacred Apis bull at the old capital of Memphis. He was perhaps even formally crowned pharaoh on or about 14 November 332 B.C. He then sailed down the River Nile and, where it meets the Mediterranean Sea, founded the first of many cities to bear the name Alexandria. In all, Alexander may have founded up to 20 such towns and cities. He personally laid out the basic plan of Egyptian Alexandria, which soon became one of the major cities of the ancient world.

His weakest link

Despite his many achievements, some historians believe that Alexander never learned to swim. Perhaps that was why he preferred to capture the Persian navy's bases on land.

November 332 B.C.
Alexander invades Egypt and is perhaps crowned pharaoh.

January 331 B.C.
Alexander founds the new city of Alexandria in Egypt.

Alexander's Campaigns

Alexander's campaigns in Asia were in four main stages.
The first, from 334 to 331 B.C., took him to Phrygia. He
went south through Phoenicia into Egypt, liberating
Greek cities from Persian rule. Along the way, he won the
crucial battles of the River Granicus and Issus. Alexander
then headed east on the second stage of his campaign,
conquering the Persian Empire and killing Bessus, the
assassin of the Persian king Darius. The next stage was
the campaign to crush opposition to his rule in central
Asia and extend his empire into India. This stage ended
when his own army mutinied against him. The final,
three-year stage of his campaign was his difficult return
from India to Babylon, where he died in 323 B.C.

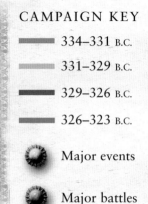

CAMPAIGN KEY

- 334–331 B.C.
- 331–329 B.C.
- 329–326 B.C.
- 326–323 B.C.

- Major events
- Major battles

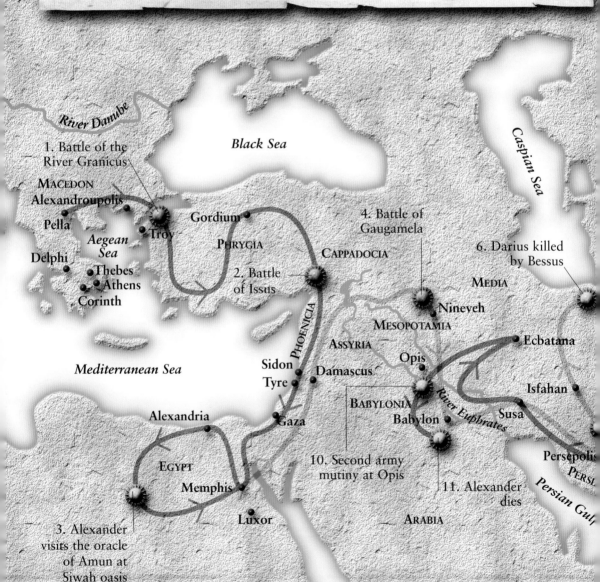

River Danube

Black Sea

1. Battle of the
River Granicus

MACEDON
Alexandroupolis

Pella

Aegean
Sea

Delphi

Troy

Gordium

PHRYGIA

Thebes
Athens
Corinth

2. Battle
of Issus

Caspian Sea

4. Battle of
Gaugamela

CAPPADOCIA

6. Darius killed
by Bessus

MEDIA

Nineveh

MESOPOTAMIA

Ecbatana

ASSYRIA

Opis

PHOENICIA

Mediterranean Sea

Sidon

Tyre

Damascus

Isfahan

River Euphrates

Susa

BABYLONIA

Alexandria

Gaza

Babylon

Persepolis

PERSI

EGYPT

10. Second army
mutiny at Opis

Memphis

11. Alexander
dies

Persian Gulf

Luxor

ARABIA

3. Alexander
visits the oracle
of Amun at
Siwah oasis

ALEXANDER'S EMPIRE

Alexander's empire stretched from Macedon in the west to the River Indus in the east, and from Egypt in the south toward the Aral Sea in the north. That is the equivalent of ruling every single country from Greece and Albania in Europe, east through Turkey, to Pakistan in Asia; and from Egypt in Africa through Israel, Jordan, Lebanon and Syria to Armenia and Azerbaijan in the Caucasus and Afghanistan and Uzbekistan in central Asia – a total of 21 modern-day countries. It was the biggest empire the world had seen.

Aral Sea

SCYTHIA

Alexandria Eschate

Bukhara

7. Bessus captured and killed

Samarkand

SOGDIANA

Bactra

PARTHIA

BACTRIA

8. Battle of the River Hydaspes

Alexandria Arachosion (Kandahar)

Hindu Kush

River Indus

River Hydaspes

PAURAVAS

Alexander burns Persepolis

ARMANIA

Pura

Gedrosian Desert

Pattala

9. Army mutiny at the River Hyphasis

N

W   E

S

INDIA

Arabian Sea

Becoming a God

Above: In Egypt, Alexander paid homage to the Egyptian gods, including the falcon-headed Horus. On this stone relief from a temple at Luxor on the Nile, he is shown wearing the crown of Egypt.

Throughout his life, Alexander was a controversial figure. He was loved, hated and feared in almost equal measure by friend and foe alike. But nothing was more controversial than his claim to be a god. He was one of the first Greeks to be worshipped as a god in his own lifetime.

While in Egypt, Alexander travelled along the Mediterranean coast and then south into the desert to consult the oracle of Amun at the Siwah oasis. The trip was doubly dangerous. Darius could have attacked while he was away, and Alexander could easily have lost his life in one of the frequent sandstorms. It is unclear why Alexander made this trip, or what questions about the future he asked at the oracle. After the visit, he always claimed a close relationship with Amun, the Egyptian sky-god.

March 331 B.C.
Alexander visits with the priest of the oracle of Amun at the Siwah oasis in Egypt.

Spring 331 B.C.
Alexander returns to Tyre and organizes the financial control of his growing Asian empire.

Alexander perhaps even believed that Amun was his father. Strange as this might seem today, claiming to be a son of a god – as opposed to claiming that you were a god – was not unusual in the Greek world. As for the Egyptians, they worshipped Alexander as a living god because he was now their pharaoh (in practice even if he was not actually crowned) and all pharaohs were divine.

Far more controversial was the occasion four years later, in 327 B.C., in Bactra (in modern-day Afghanistan) when Alexander told his court to pay 'proskynesis', or homage, to him. His new Persian subjects did not mind: they considered such homage to be a mark of respect shown to a superior, and no one was more superior than Alexander, who was by that point Great King of Persia. His Macedonian and Greek subjects, however, saw it as a religious act and many refused to obey, as they did not consider Alexander to be a god in the same way as Zeus or Apollo. But one of Alexander's reasons for demanding this homage had actually been to make his Macedonian, Greek and Persian subjects equal within his empire.

Some ancient writers have suggested that in 324 B.C. Alexander ordered everyone to worship him as a god. This cannot be proved for sure, but by now Alexander did think of himself as nearly unbeatable, and so virtually a god.

> '*The delegates ... placed golden chaplets on his head,*
> *as if their crowning were a ritual in honour of a god.*'
> **Arrian, writing about Greek delegates meeting**
> **Alexander in Babylon, spring 323 B.C.**

August 331 B.C.

Alexander and his army cross the River Euphrates into Mesopotamia.

September 331 B.C.

Alexander moves his army into Assyria and prepares to face Darius' army for the last time.

Into Persia

On 1 October 331 B.C., Alexander and his army faced Darius for their final showdown. A revolt back home in Greece had been easily crushed. Alexander was now ready to achieve his lifetime's ambition and complete his conquest of the mighty Persian Empire.

Above: Two soldiers stand at attention on the walls of Darius I's audience chamber in a palace at Persepolis.

The decisive battle took place on a hot, dusty plain at Gaugamela, not far from the old Assyrian capital of Nineveh in modern-day Iraq. Because of Darius' advantage in numbers, Alexander was advised to make a night attack. He refused, preferring to fight in daylight. Darius had around 220,000 infantry and 30,000 cavalry, while Alexander had only 40,000 infantry and 7,000 cavalry. Yet, because of better tactics and cavalry skills, Alexander won the day and Darius fled.

Autumn 331 B.C.
Antipater, Alexander's regent in Macedon, crushes a revolt by Sparta at the Battle of Megalopolis.

October 331 B.C.
King Darius' army is defeated at the Battle of Gaugamela, and Darius flees.

'I will not demean myself by stealing victory like a thief.'

Alexander to his main general, Parmenion, refusing to attack at night before the Battle of Gaugamela

After the battle, Alexander moved south through Babylonia to the great city of Babylon itself, where his army enjoyed a well-earned rest. After a month, they continued on into Persia (modern-day Iran) to the capital, Susa, where Alexander sat on the imperial golden throne for the first time. At Susa, he seized the national treasury, but more wealth was found in the royal palaces of Persepolis. There, the wealth of gold, silver, jewels, rugs, tapestries and other items was so great that a train of wagons was needed to transport it all. Then Alexander had the palaces burned to the ground.

With Persepolis burned, Alexander lost all chance of the Persians accepting him willingly as their new king. He needed to capture Darius and force him to abdicate. But as Alexander moved north towards Ecbatana, he learned that Darius had fled east toward Bactria. He made an important decision.

He decided to reorganize his army. He did not feel he could count on the loyalty of his Greek allied soldiers, who came from Greek states other than Macedon. Now that the Greek cities of Asia Minor were liberated and Darius was largely defeated, their services were no longer needed. Those who wanted to leave were paid off, while those who stayed were offered three talents, a huge sum.

The accursed thief

The Persians considered Alexander not as a hero or liberator, but as Iskander, 'the thief', for stealing their country. It is a name he is still called today in Iran.

May 330 B.C.
Alexander's army marches through the Persian Empire to Persepolis, which he burns to the ground.

June 330 B.C.
Alexander sends his Greek allied soldiers home. Those who remain are paid handsomely for their loyalty.

Having sorted out his troops, Alexander now set out at great speed in pursuit of Darius, covering 450 miles in three weeks. But his chase was in vain. Darius had been killed by a distant relative, Bessus. As the Macedonian army approached, Bessus had Darius stabbed with javelins. A Macedonian soldier found him barely alive and gave him water. By the time Alexander arrived, Darius was dead. Alexander sent his body back for burial in the royal cemetery at Persepolis and set off to capture Bessus.

Over the next three years, Alexander remained in the north of the vast Persian Empire, pursuing Bessus and then putting down rebellions in remote parts of the country. His treks took him east to what is now Kandahar, in modern Afghanistan, and then north across the Hindu Kush mountain range into central Asia. In spring 329 B.C., near Samarkand in modern Uzbekistan, he finally captured and killed Bessus. Alexander's troops fought on, conquering the entire area by 327 B.C., after a lengthy campaign.

Above: The grandeur of the Persian court at Persepolis can be seen in this surviving staircase leading up to the main Apadana, or audience chamber, of Darius' palace.

July 330 B.C.

Darius is killed by Bessus, one of his own relatives, just before Alexander can reach him.

Summer 329 B.C.

Bessus is captured and killed by Alexander in Sogdiana.

Here he showed himself to be as great a general at the small-scale, surprise attacks of guerrilla warfare as he was at large, organized battles.

By now, Alexander was behaving like a Persian emperor, not a Macedonian general. His position as king of the great Persian Empire was so important to him that he even tried to make his Macedonian troops and courtiers adopt Persian dress and customs, and pay homage to him in the Persian manner. He also married Roxane, the daughter of the defeated Sogdian chieftain whose support he wanted to buy. As far as Alexander was concerned, the conquering Macedonians should adopt the lifestyle of the defeated Persians, not the other way around.

Welling up

When Alexander was camped in Sogdiana, a spring of water and a spring of oil gushed up close to his tent. Alexander thought that this meant there was trouble ahead. In fact, it is the first mention of petroleum in all of Greek literature.

This was too much for some of his followers, who plotted against him. Alexander had already murdered one of his oldest friends, Cleitus, in a drunken brawl for daring to oppose him about this. He now turned on the conspirators, a group of royal attendants, and killed them. Alexander's chosen historian, Callisthenes, was caught up in the plot. He too was executed.

Left: In Persia, as elsewhere on his campaigns, Alexander rode on Bucephalas, by now an aging but still strong and vigorous horse.

Spring 327 B.C.
Alexander marries Roxane, and demands homage from all his subjects at Bactra, in modern-day Afghanistan.

Spring 327 B.C.
Alexander puts down the royal attendants' conspiracy against him and executes Callisthenes, his historian.

Into India

By 327 B.C., Alexander had crushed the last pockets of opposition to his rule in Persia. Many of his supporters hoped he would now rest, but Alexander had other ideas. He wanted to conquer India.

The Greeks believed that the world was surrounded by a great body of water known as 'Ocean', which lay just beyond India. Alexander longed to see this water, for then he would have conquered the entire known world. He also wanted to reconquer those parts of India that had once belonged to the Persian Empire. In the spring of 327 B.C. he recrossed the Hindu Kush into India and divided his troops. One group, under his friend Hephaestion, went east through the Khyber Pass toward the River Indus, while Alexander headed towards the more northerly hill country. The army he controlled had changed massively since the first Macedonian and allied Greek force crossed the Hellespont seven years earlier.

Below: Alexander and his army crossed the massive Hindu Kush mountain range in central Asia twice – once in pursuit of Bessus in spring 329 B.C., and then again on their way into India in spring 327 B.C.

Spring 327 B.C.
Alexander and his army recross the Hindu Kush and conquer the region of modern-day Pakistan.

Spring 327 B.C.
Alexander recruits 30,000 Persians to be trained as 'Successors' to his aging Macedonian 'Old Guard'.

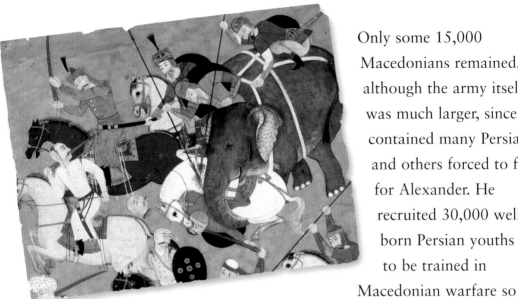

Above: During the Battle of the River Hydaspes in May 326 B.C., Alexander and his army faced terrifying war elephants.

Only some 15,000 Macedonians remained, although the army itself was much larger, since it contained many Persians and others forced to fight for Alexander. He recruited 30,000 well-born Persian youths to be trained in Macedonian warfare so that they could eventually replace his aging Macedonian 'Old Guard'. This new group he called the 'Successors'. Alexander obviously planned many more campaigns.

By spring 326 B.C., Alexander had conquered the northern Indian states and met up with Hephaestion at the River Indus. His target was now the vast lands of the raja Porus. Alexander sent a message ahead asking Porus to pay homage. Porus responded with a 50,000-strong army and 85 trained war elephants. The two armies met on either side of the River Hydaspes. But it was monsoon season, and the Hydaspes was in full flood, so Alexander could not cross. He divided his army and went upstream to find a crossing place, leaving a reserve force behind. Porus followed, Alexander crossed the river, and the two armies met. The battle was close, but Porus was defeated when Alexander's reserves crossed the river to attack Porus from behind.

May 326 B.C.

Alexander wins the Battle of the Hydaspes against Porus, raja of the Pauravas.

May 326 B.C.

Bucephalas dies of wounds received in the Battle of the Hydaspes.

Above: In his campaigns in India, Alexander used every technique he knew to capture a city, including building a wall of fire, as shown here.

It was a great victory, perhaps Alexander's finest. The defeat of Porus opened the way for the conquest of India, but Alexander's troops were tired and rain-sodden, as the monsoon continued to pour down. Alexander tried to convince them that the Ocean was near. But they had heard rumours that ahead there was just a vast land with hostile people armed with more fearsome elephants. They were reluctant to move on.

In June 326 B.C., the army moved east again to the River Hyphasis, now known as the Beas. The land was flat, and the Ocean was not in sight. At this point, the soldiers did what they had never done before – they mutinied. They refused to go any farther, and nothing Alexander said would convince them. Reluctantly, Alexander turned back to the River Hydaspes.

Some months before, Alexander had ordered the construction of a huge fleet, which was now ready on the river. Some 8,000 soldiers took to the boats and sailed down the Rivers Hydaspes and Indus toward the Arabian Sea. The rest, led by Alexander, split into two and walked down either bank. At first their march was uneventful, but soon local tribes began to attack them. The troops' march turned into one long, continuous battle.

June 326 B.C.
His army mutinies on the banks of the River Hyphasis and Alexander turns back towards the River Hydaspes.

November 326 B.C.
Some of the army begins to sail down the Rivers Hydaspes and Indus, while the rest march along the banks.

'And you may tell your people there that you deserted your king in the midst of his enemies.'

Alexander appealing for support when his army mutinied at the River Hyphasis

The Macedonians slaughtered thousands as they fought their way to the sea. At one point, Alexander besieged a town held by the Malli people. His soldiers were reluctant to join in the siege, so Alexander scrambled up a wall and into the town, urging them to follow him. Almost alone, Alexander attacked the Malli until an arrow pierced his chest. His lung was punctured, and his life in danger. Luckily, Macedonian soldiers fought their way into the town and rescued him.

Gradually Alexander recovered, and the fleet and army resumed their trek southwards, reaching Pattala (possibly modern Hyderabad) near the coast of the Arabian Sea in late summer 325 B.C. One group of older soldiers led by Craterus had already been dispatched west from the Indus toward central Persia. But now Alexander came up with perhaps the most extraordinary plan of his career – to march through the inhospitable Gedrosian (or Makran) Desert while his fleet sailed down the Indus to the sea, and then west along the Arabian Sea and into the Persian Gulf.

Left: This silver coin issued by Ptolemy I of Alexandria (304–284 B.C.) shows Alexander wearing an elephant-scalp headdress to commemorate his many victories in India.

325 B.C.
Alexander is almost killed when attacking a Malli town.

July 325 B.C.
Alexander's army and fleet reach Pattala near the Arabian Sea.

THE END OF
HIS WORLD

4

Return from India

Ever since Alexander had crossed the Hellespont all those years before, his troops had followed him faithfully into the unknown. In Pakistan, on the banks of the River Hyphasis, they had mutinied. Now, perhaps in revenge, he was to lead them into the hell of the Gedrosian Desert.

It is not known why Alexander chose the route back toward Persia that he did. He could have easily taken the more northerly and safer route already taken by Craterus and his older troops. Perhaps Alexander's reason was revenge, or perhaps it was because no one had ever walked through the Gedrosian Desert before. Whatever made him choose the route, Alexander was determined to succeed.

Alexander's plan involved close coordination between his army and the fleet led by his childhood friend Nearchus of Crete. The 85,000-strong army was to march along the shore, digging wells to provide water.

Previous page: This bronze-gilt head of Alexander was made about 100 years after his death.

Below: On their voyage along the Arabian Sea, Nearchus and his fleet sometimes encountered fishermen, like this one today, who traded them fish.

August 325 B.C.
Alexander sets out toward Persia across the terrible Gedrosian Desert.

September 325 B.C.
Nearchus reaches the Arabian Sea and begins to sail home with the fleet.

> '*The finest thing he ever did.*'
> **Arrian on Alexander refusing water in the Gedrosian Desert**

The fleet was to sail close to shore, equipped with four months' supplies. The first part of the route through what is now Baluchistan in southern Pakistan provided plentiful food and water. But then it all went wrong. The army was forced inland by coastal mountains, and it lost contact with the fleet.

The men and their women and children travelled across the fertile land until it gave way to baking hot sand with no water. At one point, a soldier found a little water and scooped it up in his helmet for Alexander to drink. Thirsty though he was, he refused to drink, sharing his men's plight. But when it rained, it poured. Every so often, the heavens opened and torrents of water ran down the dry gullies, sweeping everything away in their path. Once the rains had gone, there were sandstorms. One storm was so terrible that Alexander got lost and walked far to the north. Luckily, he realized what was happening and led a small force back to the sea. The rest of the army followed and guides discovered a road leading to the local capital, Pura, and safety. After two months, Alexander came out of the desert into southern Persia. Thousands of his men – perhaps more than half – had died of thirst and heat.

The desert trek

As the troops laboured through the Gedrosian Desert, they were attacked by venomous snakes, and their animals died after eating poisonous plants. Once, a fierce rainstorm swept away the entire baggage train, killing many women and children.

October 325 B.C.
Alexander reaches the relative safety of Pura, in southern Persia.

December 325 B.C.
Alexander, Craterus and Nearchus are reunited in southern Persia. Then Nearchus continues up the Persian Gulf toward Susa.

> 'That Persians and Macedonians might rule together in harmony as an imperial power.'
>
> **Alexander's prayer at the banquet of reconciliation in Susa, June 324 B.C.**

In Carmania, southern Persia, Alexander met up again with Craterus and the troops he had sent home from the Indus during the summer, and with Nearchus' fleet. Reunited at last, Alexander's army enjoyed huge celebrations.

But Alexander felt uneasy. Rumours were circulating about revolts and even plots against his life. He acted decisively, executing a number of his generals and satraps – both Macedonians and Persians – and ordering the rest to dismiss all mercenaries so that they could not be organized to fight against him. This was a 'reign of terror', during which Alexander acted brutally. One of his oldest friends, Harpalus, the Grand Imperial Treasurer, had just run off with a large part of Alexander's personal wealth. Alexander feared more trouble might follow.

In March 324 B.C., Nearchus ended his voyage up the Persian Gulf near Susa, where he met up with Alexander once again. Alexander took this opportunity to hold a mass wedding, awarding Persian noblewomen to more than 80 of his Macedonian followers.

Olympic uproar

At the Olympic Games in summer 324 B.C., Alexander sent orders that all Greek cities were to receive back their exiled citizens. Many of them had once fought against their own cities and fled to join Alexander. This order caused an uproar across Greece, and was to lead to a massive revolt against Macedonian rule months after Alexander's death.

January 324 B.C.
Alexander's treasurer and boyhood friend Harpalus escapes to Athens with much of Alexander's money.

January 324 B.C.
Alexander has many satraps and generals executed in a reign of terror.

He also blessed the union of 10,000 of his troops with Persian women, and gave each couple a gift of money. He himself married two women, both members of the Persian royal house, before travelling on to Opis.

Alexander's intention was to create a new Persian-Macedonian ruling class that would govern and fight for his empire in the future. However, many Macedonians objected to his continued attempts to make them adopt eastern customs. In June 324 B.C., the army mutinied again. This time, the cause was the paying-off of 10,000 Macedonian infantry and replacement of them with the 30,000 Persian 'Successors' Alexander had started to train in 327 B.C. Alexander told the mutineers to go home. Faced with this ultimatum, many backed down. Alexander held a banquet of reconciliation for his Macedonian soldiers, and gave them the Persian title 'Kinsmen'. While many of the men were reassured, many of them were not.

Below: After the baking sands of the Gedrosian Desert, these bleak hills in southern Persia must have seemed welcoming to Alexander and his troops.

April 324 B.C.
Mass weddings of Alexander and his troops with Persian women are held at Susa.

June 324 B.C.
The army mutinies again at Opis after Alexander tries to pay off his oldest and most faithful troops.

Death of a Conqueror

The last year of Alexander's life was difficult. His endless fighting, the humiliation of two army revolts, the ordeal of crossing the Gedrosian Desert, and the almost fatal wound he had received in India had drained him of much of his energy. Now he was to lose his best friend, a blow from which he would never fully recover.

Above: Alexander died in the royal palace close to the legendary Hanging Gardens of Babylon, built 250 years earlier by his Babylonian predecessor, Nebuchadrezzar.

In summer 324 B.C., Alexander travelled to his summer retreat in the hill city of Ecbatana. There he partied with friends, including his lifelong friend and companion, Hephaestion. One night, Hephaestion came down with a fever and died a few days later. Alexander was grief-stricken, cutting off his hair in mourning and ordering the manes and tails of the royal horses to be cut as well. He embalmed Hephaestion's body and sent it off to Babylon, the capital of his empire, for a lavish funeral.

Revenge for a friend

Alexander took his revenge for Hephaestion's death in the cruelest possible way, crucifying the doctor for failing to save him. He also wiped out a mountain tribe, an offering, he said, 'to the shade [spirit] of Hephaestion.'

October 324 B.C.
Alexander's best friend, Hephaestion, dies of a fever in Ecbatana, Media.

Winter 323 B.C.
Alexander arrives in Babylon and begins to plan an Arabian expedition.

After his best friend's death, Alexander threw himself into new projects, planning an invasion of Arabia and possibly even an attack on Carthage in the Mediterranean. He was 32 years old and had managed to survive everything life had thrown at him so far.

In spring 323 B.C., Alexander returned to Babylon. Seers warned him not to enter the city facing the setting sun. As there was impassable swampland west of the city, he ignored their advice and entered from the east. A series of other events – his sun hat wrapped with the royal ribbon blew against the tomb of a long-dead king, a madman sat on his throne while Alexander was on his feet reviewing troops – seemed like bad omens.

29 On May 323 B.C., Alexander held a banquet for his admiral, Nearchus of Crete, who was planning a voyage around Arabia. He continued drinking into the night and woke next day with a fever, possibly caused by typhus or malaria. His condition worsened, and he ordered his officers to remain close. He gave his royal ring to his general, Perdiccas, so that imperial business could continue to receive his seal of approval. On 10 June, friends stayed with him at his bedside. 'To whom do you leave your empire?' they asked him. 'To the strongest,' he replied. And with those words he died.

Left: Mischievously, Alexander is represented as the god Pan in this Greek marble statue. Pan was also the name given to panic in battle – something Alexander never did.

Spring 323 B.C.

Greek delegates acknowledge Alexander as a god.

10 June 323 B.C.

Alexander dies of a fever in Babylon.

Where Is Alexander Buried?

Below: This stone sarcophagus has long been associated with Alexander, but it was actually made for Nectanebo II, the last pharaoh of Egypt.

After Alexander died in Babylon in 323 B.C., his body was embalmed. The following year, a huge escort set off to take the body back to the royal cemetery at Aegae in Macedon. However, some people believed that Alexander had asked to be buried at the oracle of Amun in Egypt, which he had visited in 331. So, when the body reached Syria, Arrhidaeus, commander of the escort, changed direction and headed south through Damascus. There he was met by Ptolemy, commander of Egypt. Ptolemy took the body to Memphis, the Egyptian capital, where it remained for about 40 years until it was moved to the new capital, Alexandria. A mausoleum was built to house the body, and we know that both Julius Caesar and the first Roman emperor, Augustus, visited it. Records show that the mausoleum survived until at least A.D. 365, when an earthquake and tidal wave struck the city. The tomb and body then disappeared from history.

Below: Alexandria, Egypt, has been rebuilt many times since Alexander founded it in 331 B.C. His exact burial site has never been discovered.

HIS FINAL RESTING PLACE?

At much the same time as Alexander's body disappeared, the body of St Mark, author of one of the gospels in the Bible, first appeared in Alexandria. In A.D. 828, two merchants stole this body and took it to Venice, Italy, where a church was built to house the remains. Some people believe, however, that the body lying in St Mark's Basilica is not Mark's but Alexander's.

The Legacy of Alexander

In his short lifetime, Alexander achieved much. He was not 33 years old when he died, yet he ruled the largest empire in the world. It stretched from the Adriatic Sea in the west to what is now Pakistan in the east, and from Egypt in Africa in the south to modern Uzbekistan in central Asia in the north. But what long-term legacy did he leave?

At his death, Alexander left his empire in the hands of an unborn son by his wife Roxane and his mentally ill half-brother, Philip Arrhidaeus. Neither of these was a suitable successor. The regent, Perdiccas, tried to hold the empire together on their behalf, but by 270 B.C., three separate kingdoms had emerged, in Egypt, western Asia and Macedon itself. Eventually, each was conquered by the next great imperial power, Rome.

Below: This new library at Alexandria was founded in 2003 as a successor to the great library founded in Alexander's city. The original building was said to contain 700,000 scrolls that covered all human knowledge of the time.

323 B.C.
Alexander is succeeded by his unborn son, Alexander IV, and his half-brother. Perdiccas is regent.

321–270 B.C.
After Perdiccas is murdered, the empire eventually breaks up into three separate kingdoms.

But while Alexander's empire came under Roman rule, its Greek-speaking unity remained. Greek culture dominated his former empire until the invasion of the Arabs in the 7th century. This unity allowed Christianity to spread from its birthplace of Judaea throughout the region. Its main apostle, St Paul, was a Greek-speaker, and the New Testament was written in Greek. Without Alexander, it is unlikely that Christianity would have become a world religion.

It must also be remembered that as a leader Alexander was unsurpassed, but he was also cruel. It has been estimated that he was responsible for the deaths of three-quarters of a million people.

In 1991, the Balkan state of Yugoslavia split into independent nations. One of them, Macedonia, shares its name with a province in northern Greece. Both were once part of ancient Macedon. Greece was furious with its neighbour for using a name linked with Alexander. The two countries almost went to war on the issue – a sign of how powerful Alexander still is, more than 2,300 years after his death.

Right: This statue of Alexander on Bucephalas is in Thessaloniki in Greece, once part of ancient Macedon.

'The torch Alexander lit for long only smouldered … but it never has been, and never can be, quite put out.'
W.W. Tarn, historian and biographer of Alexander, 1948

1st century A.D.
St Paul spreads Christianity throughout the Greek-speaking world.

1991
The former Yugoslav Republic of Macedonia becomes independent, meeting with hostility from Greece.

Glossary

abdicate give up the throne, either voluntarily or under the threat of force.

Achilles hero of the Trojan Wars, son of a mortal father and a divine mother, the goddess Thetis.

Amun the Egyptian sky-god, known to the Greeks as Ammon.

Apis Egyptian sacred bull, regarded as the earthly representation of the god Ptah.

Aristotle Greek scientist and philosopher (384–322 B.C.). He was Alexander's tutor from 343 B.C.

Arrian Lucius Flavius Arrianus Xenophon, 2nd century A.D. Greek politician and intellectual who wrote two of the major surviving books about Alexander, *Anabasis* (*March Up Country*) and *Indica* (*Indian Affairs*).

aulos ancient Greek wind instrument with a double reed.

besiege surround a city with an army in order to force it to surrender.

bust (a sculpture) a piece of sculpture representing the head, shoulders, and upper chest of a human body.

Callisthenes relative of Aristotle appointed by Alexander to be his official historian. He was implicated in a plot against Alexander and executed for treason in 327 B.C.

campaign to undertake military actions, such as a series of raids or invasions.

cavalry troops mounted on horses.

city-state state consisting of an independent city and its surrounding territory.

class group of people of similar social and economic status.

courtier member of a royal court who works for the king.

Delphic oracle shrine of the god Apollo at Delphi in central Greece where a priestess resided who was believed to utter only divine truths.

dialect form of language spoken in a particular geographical area.

Dionysus Greek god of wine and transformation.

embalm to treat a dead body with preservatives to keep it from decaying.

envoy diplomat, representative or messenger sent by one state to another.

grand vizier chief officer or personal minister of a king or emperor.

guerrilla warfare warfare fought by small, irregular groups of soldiers using their local knowledge to great advantage.

heir male or female successor to the throne after the death or resignation of a monarch.

Heracles son of the god Zeus and a mortal woman, Alcmene, he was famous for his 12 superhuman labours. Known also by his Roman name, Hercules.

homage show of respect to a superior.

Homer blind poet considered to have composed the *Iliad*, about the Trojan War, and the *Odyssey*, about the lengthy travels of Odysseus after the war. Seven Greek cities claimed to be the birthplace of Homer, but nothing is known of his life or dates, and it is unlikely that one person alone composed either text.

infantry the part of the army made up of soldiers who fight on foot.

lyre ancient Greek stringed instrument with a tortoise shell for a sounding box, the strings of which were plucked.

mausoleum a large, stately tomb.

mercenary soldier who fights for a foreign country or ruler for money.

mutiny open rebellion by soldiers against their commander.

Olympic Games Greek games held in Olympia once every four years in ancient times, traditionally believed to have started in 776 B.C.

omen event that is regarded as a sign of future happiness or disaster.

oracle shrine at which a priest or priestess reveals divine messages and statements.

pharaoh the title given to the king and supreme ruler of ancient Egypt.

proskynesis Greek word for the religious act of worship performed solely to the gods. Persians considered proskynesis to be merely a social custom, an act of respect or homage to a social superior with no religious meaning.

Plutarch Greek philosopher and biographer (c. 46–120 A.D.) famous for his *Fifty Parallel Lives*, in which he compares pairs of Greek and Roman soldiers and statesmen. He paired Alexander with Julius Caesar.

regent person in charge of governing a country when the king or queen is too young, or when they are absent.

royal house a royal family.

sarcophagus a stone coffin, often decorated with carvings.

satrap local governor of a satrapy, or region, of the Persian Empire.

seer person who claims to be able to see into the future.

stallion male horse, often used for breeding.

symposium Greek all-male drinking party at which politics and other issues were discussed.

treason serious offence against the king, queen or government of a country, usually punishable by death.

Trojan Wars mythical wars between the Greeks and the city of Troy in Asia Minor, caused by the abduction of the Greek queen Helen by Paris, son of King Priam of Troy. The wars lasted ten years, and were possibly based on a real war or wars that took place c. 1200 B.C.

Bibliography

Alexander the Conqueror: The Epic Story of the Warrior King, Foreman, Laura, published by Da Capo Press, 2004

Alexander the Great: The Heroic Ideal, Briant, Pierre, published by Thames & Hudson, 1996

Alexander the Great: The Hunt for a New Past, Cartledge, Paul, published by Macmillan, 2004. The author of this book is particularly indebted to Professor Cartledge for bringing Alexander so much to life in his excellent work of biography and historical investigation.

History Today, July 2004, Volume 54 (7). For an article by Paul Cartledge about Alexander, and one by Andrew Chugg about the whereabouts of his tomb.

Some websites that will help you explore Alexander's life:

wso.williams.edu:8000/~junterek
A website about Alexander packed with information about him, his parents, his youth and his brilliant empire-building campaigns in Asia.

www.pothos.org
Contains extensive information about Alexander with sections on his animals, art and legends, battles and campaigns, his contemporaries and his death.

www.isidore-of-seville.com/ImagesofAlexander
A visual look at Alexander, with more than 200 images from antiquity to the present.

www.angelfire.com/il/AlexanderTheGreat
Information about Alexander, his parents, his tutor Aristotle and his battles, with a lengthy timeline.

www.e-classics.com/ALEXANDER.htm
Read Plutarch's life of Alexander, in an abridged modern English version.

Index

Achilles 9, 23
Aegae 10, 33, 56
Alexander III 2, 3
  and father 8, 9, 12–13, 24–25
  appearance 19, 20
  as god 38–39
  as Great King of Persia 39
  as pharaoh 35, 38, 39
  as regent 20, 24
  becomes king 24, 25
  birth of 8–9, 10
  burial site 56–57
  character 20, 21, 27, 28, 32, 59
  conspiracy against 43
  death of 36, 47, 52, 54–55, 58
  education 17, 20–21, 22–23
  health 8, 20
  in Egypt 35, 38–39
  in India 44–47

  injury 47
  in Persia 40–43
  military campaigns 24, 28, 32–33, 36–47, 43, 45, 46, 54
  mutinies against 36, 37, 46–47, 50, 53
  naming 8, 9
  pursuit of Darius 41, 42
  reign of terror 52
  religion 21
  sieges 32, 33, 34, 35
  skills 17, 21
  sports 17, 21
  tests of manhood 16–17, 20
  tutors 15, 17, 20, 22
  wives 26, 27, 43
Alexander IV 26, 58
Alexandria, cities called 35
Alexandria, Egypt 35, 36, 56, 58

Alexandroupolis 25, 36
Amun
  as Alexander's supposed father 39
  oracle of 27, 36, 38
Amyntas 12
animals 17, 22
  bears 17
  horses 8, 9, 14–15, 20
  lions 17, 24
  snakes 21
  war elephants 45
  wild boar 16, 17
Arabia 55
Arabian Sea 37, 46, 47, 50
Aral Sea 37
Aristotle 16, 20, 22–23, 27
Arrhidaeus, commander 56
Arsites 32
Artaxerxes III 27

Asia 28, 29, 32, 33, 36–37,
    42, 58
Asia Minor 25, 26, 32, 36, 41
Assyria 36, 39
Athens 10, 12, 22, 24, 25, 35
Augustus, Roman Emperor 56

Babylon 36, 38, 41, 54, 55
    Hanging Gardens of 54
Babylonia 41
Bactra (city) 37, 39, 43
Bactria (region) 37, 41
Bagoas 27
battles
    Chaeronea 24
    Gaugamela 36, 40, 41
    Issus 32, 33, 34, 36
    Megalopolis 40
    River Granicus 32, 36
    River Hydaspes 15, 37, 45
Bessus 36, 37, 42, 44
Bucephalas 14–15, 32, 43,
    45, 59
Byzantium 10, 24

Caligula 15
Callisthenes 43
Carmania 37, 52
Carthage 55
Chalcidice 10, 13
Cleitus 33, 43
Cleopatra, Alexander's sister 25
Companion Cavalry 11, 24
Craterus 47, 50, 51, 52

Darius III 26, 27, 32, 33, 38,
    39, 40–41
    death of 36, 42
Delphi 10, 12, 20, 36
    oracle 12, 20, 21
Demosthenes 20

Ecbatana 27, 36, 41, 54
Egypt 13, 35, 36, 37, 38–39, 58

Gaza, siege of 34, 35
Gedrosian Desert 37, 47,
    50–51, 53, 54

gods and goddesses
    Amun 27–28, 38, 39
    Dionysus 21
    Zeus 8
Gordian knot 28, 29, 33
Gordium 29, 36
Greece 10, 12, 24, 28, 40, 52,
    58, 59
    city-states 10, 12, 25
    global influence 59
    language 10

Halicarnassus 10, 32, 33
Harpalus 52
Helios Kosmokrator 2
Hellespont 10, 28, 29, 44, 50
Hephaestion 26, 27, 44, 45
    death of 27, 54–55
Heracles 8
Hercules *see* Heracles
Hindu Kush 37, 42, 44
Homer 9, 23
hunting 16, 17

Illyria 8, 10, 28
India 15, 26, 36, 37, 44–47,
    50, 54
Ionia 10, 33

Julius Caesar 56

Khyber Pass 44

League of Corinth 25, 26,
    27, 28
Leonidas 17, 14
Lysimachus 15, 17

Macedon 8, 9, 10–11, 12, 14,
    20, 24, 28, 34, 36, 37,
    40, 58, 59
    and enemies 8
    as city-state 10
    capital Pella 9, 10, 11, 24
    court 16
    palaces 11, 24
Macedonia (Former Yugoslav
    Republic) 59

Macedonian Foot Companions
    11
Malli people 47
mass weddings 52, 53
Mediterranean Sea 35, 55
Memphis 35, 56
Mesopotamia 36, 39
Miletus 10, 32, 33

Nearchus of Crete 50, 51,
    52, 55
Nebuchadrezzar 54

Olympia 9, 10
Olympias
    and Alexander 8, 9, 12,
        13, 21
    and Philip 8, 9, 12, 13
    as priestess 21
Olympic Games 9, 21, 52
Opis 36, 53
Oxyartes 26

Paris 9
Parmenion 8, 26, 41
Pattala 37, 47
Perdiccas, Alexander's general
    55, 58
Perdiccas III 12
Persepolis 36, 40, 41, 42
Persian Empire 2, 21, 24, 25,
    26, 27, 32, 36, 40–43, 44,
    45, 47
    capital Susa 36, 41
    navy 34, 35
Persian Gulf 47, 51
Philip II
    and Alexander 8, 15, 17,
        22, 24–25
    and Olympias 9, 25
    army 11
    as regent 12
    assassination of 25
    birth of 10
    marriages 8, 9, 13
    military campaigns 8, 11,
        12, 16, 20, 24, 25
    tomb 12, 13

Philip III Arrhidaeus 13, 26, 58
Phoenicia 33, 34, 36
plants 22
Plutarch 8, 9, 17
Porus, raja 45, 46
Ptolemy, commander of Egypt
    47, 56
Pura 37, 51

Richard III of England 15
rivers
    Danube 28, 36
    Euphrates 36, 39
    Hydaspes 37, 46
    Hyphasis 37, 46, 47, 50
    Indus 37, 46, 47, 52
    Nile 35
    Oxus 42

Rome, Italy 58
Roxane 26, 27, 43, 58

sacrifices 35, 54
St. Paul 58, 59
sarcophagi 2, 56
Sogdiana 26, 37, 42
Sparta 10, 12, 40
Spithridates, satrap of Ionia 33
sports 9
    athletics 17
    chariot racing 9
    running 9, 17
    wrestling 9
'Successors', the 44, 45, 53
Susa 36, 51, 52, 53
symposia 16, 17
Syria 56

Thebes 10, 12, 28, 29
    rebellion of 28
Thrace 10, 16, 21
    Maedi 17, 24, 25
Thessaloniki 59
Thessaly 10, 12, 17
Troy 10, 32
Tyre 34, 36, 38

Venice, Italy 56

wars
    Fourth Sacred War 24
    Third Sacred War 12, 14
    Trojan Wars 9, 23

Acknowledgments

Source: AA = The Art Archive.

B = bottom, C = centre, T = top.

Front cover AA/Dagli Orti; **1** AA/Dagli Orti; **3** AA/Dagli Orti; **4T** Scala, Florence/Museo Archeologico, Syracuse; **4B** AA/Dagli Orti; **5T** AA/Dagli Orti; **5B** AA/Dagli Orti; **7** Scala, Florence/Museo Archeologico, Syracuse; **8** AA/Dagli Orti; **9** AA/Dagli Orti; **10–11** Getty Images/Altrendo; **11T** akg-images/Peter Connolly; **11B** Corbis/© John Heseltine; **12** AA/Dagli Orti; **13T** AA/Dagli Orti; **13B** AA/Dagli Orti; **14** Scala, Florence/Museo Archeologico, Florence; **16** Scala, Florence/Museo Archeologico, Chiusi; **17** AA/Dagli Orti; **19** AA/Dagli Orti; **20** Scala, Florence; **22** The Bridgeman Art Library/Galleria Spada, Rome; **23T** AA/Dagli Orti; **23B** AA/Dagli Orti; **24** AA/Dagli Orti; **26** AA/Dagli Orti; **29** Scala, Florence/ Castel Sant'Angelo, Rome; **31** AA/Dagli Orti; **32** Scala, Florence/Museo Nazionale, Naples; **33** AA/Dagli Orti; **34** Corbis/© Carmen Redondo; **37** AA/Dagli Orti; **38** AA/Dagli Orti; **40** AA/Dagli Orti; **42** AA/ Dagli Orti; **43** AA/Dagli Orti; **44** Corbis/© Julian Calder; **45** Corbis/© Stapleton Collection; **46** Ancient Art & Architecture Collection; **47** AA; **49** AA/Dagli Orti; **50** Corbis/© Bojan Brecelj; **53** Corbis/© Paul Almasy; **54** Corbis/© Bettmann; **55** AA/Dagli Orti; **56C** Andrew Chugg; **56B** Getty Images/Stone; **57** Scala, Florence; **58** Katz/Gamma; **59** Getty Images/Taxi.